THE PITKIN GUIDE

TOLKIEN

Robert S. Blackham

J.R.R. TOLKIEN was one of the most imaginative, remarkable and influential authors of the 20th century. Two of his works – *The Hobbit* and *The Lord of the Rings* – are now regarded as masterpieces of fantasy literature, epic visions that have entertained millions of people through either the written word or their film depictions. His books have been translated into over 40 languages.

Literature is the thread that runs throughout Tolkien's colourful, difficult life. Both his parents had died by the time he was 12, yet a lively mind survived the tragedy, and as a young man he began to learn other languages and became interested in Norse mythology. In 1916, shortly after his marriage, he was plunged into the horror of the First World War, participating in the Battle of the Somme, but he also began the long process of writing and creating the fictional world of Middle-earth.

Following the war, his academic talents secured him a career in university teaching – most of his adult life was spent as a professor at Oxford. There he was active within the thriving literary scene, and wrote many of the works for which he is renowned. These not only included his great fantasy novels, but also works of poetry, literary criticism, philosophy and translation.

From the 1960s, Tolkien's writing brought him a level of fame he often did not want. His death in 1973 only intensified this fame, and many of his books were published posthumously. The hugely popular film adaptations of his works have spread Tolkien's name and vision through a much wider audience. Some four decades after Tolkien's death, interest in his works is ever-growing and reaching new generations.

EARLY DAYS

John Ronald Reuel (J.R.R.) Tolkien (he preferred to be called Ronald) was born on 3 January 1892 in Bloemfontein in the Orange Free State in southern Africa. His parents were Arthur, manager of the Bank of Africa in Bloemfontein, and Mabel Tolkien; they had married in Cape Town in 1891, and Ronald was their first child. Ronald's brother, Hilary, was born on 17 February 1894.

Ronald would spend less than four years in southern Africa, but even this period left its mark in his later writings. His experience of being bitten by a large spider possibly informed later creations, such as Shelob in *The Two Towers* volume of *The Lord of the Rings* trilogy. In the same work, large elephant-like creatures feature in the form of Oliphaunts, a name similar to the Afrikaans for 'elephant'.

Mabel had family roots back in Birmingham in the UK, and she and her two sons returned to England for a visit in the spring of 1895, staying with her parents in Ashfield Road, King's Heath. It was while there that Ronald suffered the first major tragedy of his life. In November, Arthur Tolkien, still in Africa, became ill with rheumatic fever. He remained in poor health for some months, then had a severe haemorrhage on 14 February 1896. He died the following day.

Mabel Tolkien and her boys now had to cope on their own, with a modest income, and the next few years would be a time of real economic hardship. In the summer of 1896, they rented 5 Gracewell Cottages on Wake Green Road, in the small hamlet of Sarehole, on the rural edge of industrial Birmingham. Despite the

ABOVE: Number 5 Gracewell Cottages, home to Mabel, Ronald and Hilary Tolkien from 1896 to 1900.

RIGHT: Sarehole Mill, the view as it would have been seen from the front doorway of 5 Gracewell Cottages by the Tolkien family.

loss of his father, this became a golden time for Ronald Tolkien, who grew to love the countryside around him.

In 1900, Ronald passed his examination for King Edward's School in New Street, in Birmingham city centre. Travelling from Sarehole was a problem without public transport, so Mabel decided to move to Moseley Village to access the steam-tram system. Moving from rural to urban living was a big change for Ronald, one not to his liking. Yet even more relocations were to come. After a very short time in Moseley, the family moved to Westfield Road on the Grange Estate, King's Heath, then to Oliver Road in Edgbaston. Here he attended the Birmingham Oratory Church, where the family became friendly with Father Francis Xavier Morgan, the local parish priest.

It was during this time that tragedy visited the young boy once again. In 1904, Mabel became ill with diabetes. She spent some time in hospital, then the family moved just outside Birmingham and stayed in Hillside Cottage, in the large grounds of Oratory House in Rednal, which was a retreat for the Oratory priests. Mabel's diabetes overcame her, and she died in November.

After a short time Ronald and his brother returned to Edgbaston to live with their aunt, Beatrice Suffield, in Stirling Road. However, the boys did not settle satisfactorily and in 1908 they moved from Stirling Road to Duchess Road, to Mrs Faulkner's boarding house. She held musical evenings attended by some of the priests from the Oratory. Living at Duchess Road at the time was Edith Bratt, also an orphan, and romance started to blossom between Ronald and Edith. This relationship was frowned on by Father Francis, who had become Ronald and Hilary's guardian after Mabel's death. The brothers were consequently moved out of Duchess Road into a house in Highfield Road, and Ronald was banned from seeing Edith until he came of age at 21.

RIGHT: The Ivy Bush pub, which Tolkien would have passed on his way to school each day. The Ivy Bush Tavern appears in chapter one of *The Lord of the Rings*.

ABOVE: Perrot's Folly tower in Edgbaston, Birmingham, thought locally to be the inspiration for Minus Morgul or Minas Tirith, two of the towers in *The Lord of the Rings*.

FAIRYTALES and DRAGONS

At Sarehole, Mabel Tolkien home-schooled her sons, encouraging their appetite for learning with a wide variety of literature. She gave Ronald storybooks such as *Alice's Adventures in Wonderland* and *The Pied Piper of Hamelin*, but his special book was *The Red Fairy Book* by Andrew Lang. His favourite story was about Sigurd, who killed dragons, and who inspired him to write his own stories about these mythical creatures. Mabel also instructed the boys in Latin, art and botany, subjects that would persist as influences in Tolkien's life and writing. Alongside Mabel's education, Sarehole itself also inspired the young Tolkien, there being many wonderful places to see and explore in the countryside around the hamlet.

STUDENT DAYS

In December 1910, Tolkien embarked on the beginning of what would be a long academic career. He took his entrance examinations for the University of Oxford, and in October 1911 began his attendance at Exeter College.

Exeter College was an all-male institution (women were not admitted until 1978) that stood on Broad Street and Turl Street in the heart of Oxford. Tolkien's poor background meant he entered the college as a scholarship student; many of his fellow students would have come from public schools and affluent backgrounds. His bedroom and sitting room looked out onto Turl Street and were in the college building known as the 'Swiss Cottage' (this building was demolished in 1964).

Here Tolkien settled into the curious life of Oxford education, very different from his previous experiences. His name was painted on a board in the hall leading to the stairs to his rooms, and he even had a servant, known as a 'scout', who would bring him his breakfast. Tolkien threw himself into college life, playing rugby and joining a number of university societies. His literary interests also developed further. He was reading Classics, but became bored with Latin and Greek and focused more on Germanic literature. He also took Comparative Philology under the tutelage of Joseph Wright. Wright had risen from inauspicious beginnings (he had started work in a

mill in Yorkshire aged six) to reach the heights of academic achievement, and was an inspiration to all who studied under him.

Tolkien was a diligent student, although he could be boisterous like many other young men. On one occasion he hijacked a horse-drawn tram (there were no engine-powered buses till 1912) when the students were 'ragging' the town. The tram filled up with students, but Tolkien then abandoned it at Carfax Tower and roused a mob of students with a speech. He walked on to St Giles, and from the steps of the Martyrs' Memorial Tolkien again addressed a crowd of students and 'townies' (townsfolk).

In 1913, at the age of 21, Tolkien renewed his relationship with his childhood sweetheart Edith Bratt. He also took his Honour Moderation examinations, but failed to get the much-desired First Class result. Dr Farnell, the head of Exeter College, knowing of Tolkien's interest in Old English and Germanic languages, arranged for him to switch subjects, so that he could study English Language and Literature, specializing in

ABOVE: The Fellows' Garden, Exeter College, with the Radcliffe Camera's dome on the right and the Bodleian Library on the left.

Old Norse. The change evidently suited Tolkien's aptitudes and interests. Tolkien took his final examinations at the Sheldonian Theatre on Broad Street in June 1915, and achieved a First Class Honours degree.

LEFT: Students 'ragging the town', which usually involved high spirits, mischief and mayhem.

ROMANCE with EDITH

The great love of Tolkien's life was Edith Mary Tolkien, née Bratt, born in January 1889 in Gloucestershire. Like Tolkien, Edith was orphaned at an early age, and the two met when Ronald was 16 and Edith was 19. Their relationship was temporarily prohibited by Tolkien's guardian, Father Francis, but the romance nevertheless endured. On 3 January 1913 – Tolkien's 21st birthday – he wrote to Edith, and went to see her in Cheltenham five days later. After just a single day spent together, the couple decided to marry, an event that involved Edith breaking off an existing engagement to be married. Their wedding took place three years later, after Edith had converted to Tolkien's Roman Catholic faith. The marriage was a long and happy one, and the couple were devoted to each other, and to their children and grandchildren.

The War Years

By October 1914, at the beginning of the Michaelmas term, Tolkien found Oxford much changed. The First World War had been raging for two months, and the number of new students had fallen as men joined the armed services in their thousands. Oxford's grandest college, Christ Church, had been taken over by the Oxford Hussars, and Balliol, Keble and other colleges were similarly occupied by units of the Territorial Force. The Examination Schools and later Radcliffe Infirmary and Somerville College became military hospitals; convalescing soldiers, in their distinctive blue uniforms, filled the streets during the daytime.

Tolkien had initially decided to carry on with his studies, but his brother Hilary had joined the army in September 1914, becoming a drummer and bugler in the 3rd Birmingham Battalion. Although a military musician, on active service his main job was that of a stretcher bearer, a dangerous duty which he performed throughout the war.

Tolkien himself, who by now had rooms in St John Street, also felt the pull of army service. He joined the Officers' Training Corps and was soon undertaking army drill exercises in the University Parks, a short walk from his rooms. His official military career, however, began in the summer of 1915 when he took up a commission as a second lieutenant in the 13th Lancashire Fusiliers. His training began in Bedford, in De Pary's Avenue, and then he moved to Rugeley and Brocton Camps on Cannock Chase in Staffordshire, where he was instructed in the basic tactics of trench warfare. In early 1916 he started training as a signals officer, a duty that most likely suited the linguistically trained young man, and he became the battalion signals officer.

RIGHT: Tolkien wearing his officer's uniform. He served in the Lancashire Fusiliers during the Battle of the Somme.

LOVE'S SONG and DANCE

In 1917 Tolkien was based in an army camp in Yorkshire and Edith was living nearby, in the village of Roos. When Tolkien was given leave from the camp, he and Edith would often go on long walks. On one such walk, they came across a wood with an understorey of hemlock. Edith sang and danced for her husband on the woodland floor. Inspired by this interlude in the woodland, Tolkien wrote *The Tale of Beren and Lúthien*, where the mortal man Beren falls in love with Lúthien, an immortal elven-maid. This theme became central to Tolkien's *The Silmarillion*, a large collection of mythopeoic tales that Tolkien began in 1914 and worked on sporadically for the next four decades. Tolkien considered himself as Beren and Edith was Lúthien, and the tale also illustrates the tender love the couple had for one another. The book, however, remained unpublished until after his death.

A posting to France was imminent, but before that occurred Tolkien had one important duty to perform. On 22 March 1916, he married Edith Bratt at St Mary Immaculate Church in Warwick. They honeymooned in Clevedon in North Somerset. They had only been married for just over two months before the inevitable happened – Ronald left for France, and war, on 4 June 1916.

Tolkien arrived in France on 6 June. It was an inauspicious time to be sent to the Western Front. The Battle of the Somme started on 1 July, and Tolkien's battalion moved to the village of Bouzincourt, where it was held in reserve. Tolkien's immediate unit – B Company (he was now in the 11th Battalion) – was sent 'up the line' on the morning of 14 July, marching off into the Ancre Valley towards Albert, where they skirted around the now badly damaged edges of the town. They went into action in an attack on the ruined village of Ovillers, still in the hands of the German army.

Tolkien's later writings would have an acute sense of the horrors of combat, which he experienced during the Somme battles. After a few days of continuous fighting with little or no sleep, he returned to Bouzincourt. Life for Tolkien and the men in B Company now settled into a strange routine, with days of fighting in the trenches interspersed with rest behind the lines. In late September, his company was involved in the battle for the Schwaben Redoubt, a German fortification close to the village of Thiepval, where the fighting was particularly intense.

Then, in late November, with the Somme campaign coming to an end, Tolkien came down with trench fever, a lice-borne disease affecting soldiers on both sides of the front line. It was possibly his salvation. He was shipped back to England to the First Southern Military Hospital (located in Birmingham University). By the third week of December, he was able to leave hospital and go to Great Haywood, close to Brocton Camp, where he and Edith rented a cottage, and where he started writing *The Book of Lost Tales*. He never went overseas to fight again.

AFTER the WAR

I n October 1918, Tolkien was out of hospital again. Trench fever had plagued his health for the past two years, and with the war drawing to a close he went to Oxford to look for work. He contacted William Craigie, who had taught him Icelandic, and who at the time was working on the *Oxford English Dictionary*. William offered him a job, so Tolkien became an assistant lexicographer, working mainly on words beginning with the letter 'W'. His work was undertaken in the Old Ashmolean Building on Broad Street, next door to Exeter College.

The war ended on 11 November 1918, and Tolkien contacted the army authorities to seek permission to stay in Oxford until his demobilization. He took rooms at 50 St John Street, and Edith and their infant son, John, born the previous year, joined him there later in November. In the summer of 1919, they rented a small house in Alfred Street (now Pusey Street), just round the corner from St John Street.

To supplement his income, Tolkien was also working as a private tutor in Anglo-Saxon, mainly teaching the young ladies from the women's colleges such as Lady Margaret Hall. (As he was

BELOW: Turl Street looking towards Broad Street with Exeter College on the right.

ROVERANDOM

One surviving work from Tolkien's period in Yorkshire is *Roverandom*, which is believed to have its origins from the Tolkien's family holiday in the town of Filey, on the Yorkshire coast, in 1925. Michael Tolkien, almost five at the time, had a small toy dog of which he was very fond, but sadly this was lost on the beach. Tolkien created the story as a way of explaining the dog's disappearance. It focused on the adventures of a dog named Rover, who bit a wizard who then changed him into a toy dog. The remainder of the tale involves Rover's attempt to return to his true form. The story was not published until 1998.

RIGHT: The cover of *Roverandom*, a story first told in 1925.

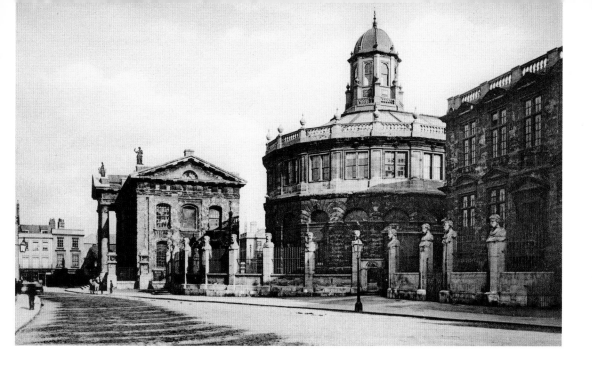

a married man living with his wife, the ladies could attend tuition at his house without a chaperone.) By the spring of 1920, this work was bringing in enough money to allow him to give up his work on the dictionary. Things were about to change, however. His second son, Michael, was born in October 1920, and Tolkien was appointed to the position of Reader in English Language at Leeds University. He and his family now moved to Leeds, where they would stay until 1925.

The Tolkiens lived at 11 St Marks Terrace, close to the university. During his time at Leeds, Tolkien and philologist E.V. Gordon, who also worked at the university and established the combined teaching of Old and Modern Icelandic there, formed a club for undergraduates, where they would drink copious quantities of beer and read sagas. It was called, appropriately enough, the Viking Club. Tolkien and Gordon became great friends and shared a common interest in Norse languages; they published a new edition of *Sir Gawain and The Green Knight* in 1925. Tolkien also discovered his gift as a storyteller while enthralling his sons with stories to help them go to sleep.

ABOVE: The Clarendon Building (left), the Sheldonian Theatre (centre) and the Old Ashmolean Building (right) on Broad Street.

LEFT: Leeds University where Tolkien taught from 1920–25, before returning to Oxford.

RETURN to OXFORD

Tolkien returned to Oxford from Leeds in 1925, having been elected Rawlinson and Bosworth Professor of Anglo-Saxon. He was contracted to give 36 lectures a year, but usually gave at least twice this number, in order to cover the topics of Anglo-Saxon and Middle English comprehensively.

Tolkien was appointed to Pembroke College, but taught students from other colleges. (Professors at Oxford teach on a faculty basis, but are given a college fellowship so they have the support and social life of a college.) Tolkien held this position until 1945, and *The Hobbit* and much of *The Lord of the Rings* were written during this period of his life.

In 1925 Tolkien bought 22 Northmoor Road, in north Oxford. It was a well-placed location – the house is close to the River Cherwell and the University Parks, and a short cycle-ride from the centre of the city. For Tolkien, this meant that he would be able to pop home, between lectures or meetings, for lunch. The whole Tolkien family returned from Leeds and moved into the house in early 1926, they lived there until 1930. At this point they moved next door to number 20, and stayed at this address until 1947.

Tolkien's life at Northmoor Road was that of a middle-class family man, living in a leafy suburb. His third son, Christopher, had been born in Leeds in November 1924, and his only daughter, Priscilla, was born in 1929.

BELOW LEFT: Lady Margaret Hall seen from the banks of the River Cherwell. Tolkien's home was nearby and he taught female students from the college after the First World War.

BELOW RIGHT: Pembroke College seen from the entrance to Pembroke Square. Tolkien lectured in Anglo-Saxon and Middle English from 1925–45 when he was a Fellow of Pembroke College.

THE FATHER CHRISTMAS LETTERS

In 1920, while still at Leeds, Tolkien started what was to become a series of letters to his children from Father Christmas at the North Pole. These were written in shaky style to disguise his handwriting from the children. Over the years, the number of characters in the letters expanded to include a polar bear, a gardener snowman, snow-elves and a gang of mischievous goblins. The letters were published in 1976 under the title *The Father Christmas Letters*.

LEFT: Punts on the River Cherwell. Tolkien enjoyed the quiet upper reaches of the river.

The three boys went to school a short distance away – the institution was fittingly titled Dragon School. The Tolkiens employed Icelandic au pairs to help around the house. Edith had an aviary where she kept canaries and budgerigars, and in his spare time Tolkien grew vegetables in the garden; in the Second World War, the family also kept chickens in the garden to ensure a fresh supply of eggs during rationing.

The years in Oxford appear to have been a happy time. Reaffirming his mother's tuition in botany, Tolkien started drawing landscapes and trees again, something he had enjoyed doing in his youth. In this pursuit he was much influenced by the style of Arthur Rackham, whose representations of trees informed the character of Old Man Willow in *The Lord of the Rings*.

Tolkien often demonstrated high spirits – sometimes on New Year's Eve, he would dress up as an Anglo-Saxon warrior or a polar bear and chase his neighbours. He also occasionally kept a barrel of

beer in the coal-hole, most likely to keep it cool, but Edith would complain that it made the house smell like a brewery.

The Tolkiens hired a punt each year and would go on expeditions down the River Cherwell, passing the University Parks alongside the long narrow island called Mesopotamia. They typically spent their holidays in Britain, and Father Francis, Tolkien's guardian after his mother Mabel died, would often come on holiday with the family. Father Francis died on 11 June 1935 and left Ronald and his brother £1,000 each in his will, in those days quite a large sum of money.

As well as being a family man, Tolkien was also an affable and popular lecturer. Students would come to the houses in Northmoor Road for tutorials in his study, and he would cycle to college to give lectures with both his gown and briefcase in the basket on the front of the bicycle.

FAR RIGHT: 20 Northmoor Road, the Tolkien family home in north Oxford, from 1930 to 1947.

RIGHT: A blue plaque commemorates Tolkien's residence at 20 Northmoor Road, Oxford.

OXFORDSHIRE BLUE PLAQUES BOARD

J.R.R.TOLKIEN

Author of
The Lord of the Rings

Lived here
1930 - 1947

OXFORD CIVIC SOCIETY

EARLY WRITING

The period from his late teens until the 1930s was a highly productive one for Tolkien in terms of his writing. These years laid the foundations of his future achievements. His talent with languages – an evident interest from his earliest childhood – was already undeniable. Even by his late teens, he already had a firm grasp of Latin and Greek, and had begun work on Northern European languages such as Gothic and Finnish. Further back in his childhood, while living in King's Heath, he acquired an interest in the Welsh language, on account of the colliery names painted on coal wagons seen on the railway line behind his home. His vivid imagination led to him inventing his own languages, with their own grammar, to entertain himself.

Tolkien expressed his love of literature socially as well as privately. In his senior years at King Edward's School in Birmingham, Tolkien and other pupils formed a club called the Tea Club Barrovian Society, better known as the 'T.C.B.S.'. Tolkien would read from *Beowulf* to the other members of the club, indicating his keen interest in Norse sagas. Inspired by one of his English literature teachers, 'Dickie' Reynolds, Tolkien also started to write verse while still at school.

BELOW: Tolkien admired Arthur Rackham's drawings. This illustration by Rackham is of *The trees and the axe* from *Aesop's Fables*, c. 1912.

Poetry was an early and enduring love for Tolkien. In the September of 1914, for example, he went to stay with his Aunt Jane at Phoenix Farm in Gedling, Nottinghamshire. Aunt Jane was the younger sister of his mother and was a great influence on Tolkien's life up until her death in 1963. While staying at the farm, Tolkien started writing the poem 'The Voyage of Eärendel the Evening Star'. Eärendel would go on to become an important character in Tolkien's lifelong work *The Silmarillion*. Other poems written around this time included 'The Bidding of the Minstrel' (1914), 'Tinfang Warble' (1914), 'You and Me / and the Cottage of Lost Play' (1915), 'Over Old Hills and Far Away' (1915) and 'Habbanan beneath the Stars' (1916).

As well as writing poetry, Tolkien was a prolific academic writer. In 1922 he published *A Middle English Vocabulary*, and three years later co-edited the 14th-century romance *Sir Gawain and*

RIGHT: *The Adoration of the Magi*, a hand-woven wool tapestry made by William Morris and Company, and designed by Edward Burne-Jones, hangs in Exeter College Chapel. Tolkien was a great enthusiast of Morris.

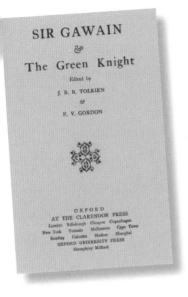

LEFT: Frontispiece from *Sir Gawain and The Green Knight*, the medieval romance which Tolkien edited and published with E.V. Gordon.

The Green Knight with E.V. Gordon. These were just the first two of some 20 academic works published between 1920 and the mid 1960s, and they show the range of Tolkien's intellectual talents.

The influences on Tolkien's early works were extremely broad, and stemmed from both personal experience and literary preferences. The countryside was always significant. In a rare interview in 1966, reproduced in *The Guardian* newspaper in 1991, Tolkien described how important the little hamlet of Sarehole had been in the development of his fictional vision: 'It was a kind of lost paradise ... There was an old mill that really did grind corn with two millers, a great big

ABOVE: Coal wagons inscribed with Welsh names, seen on the railway near his home in King's Heath, Birmingham, intrigued Tolkien as a boy.

IMPRESSIONS of WAR

In later life, Tolkien was somewhat dismissive of claims that he had begun writing his great fantastical works in the trenches of the First World War. He observed, 'You might scribble something on the back of an envelope and shove it in your back pocket, but that's all. You couldn't write ... you'd be crouching down amongst flies and filth.' He agreed that the powerful impressions of war took hold at a 'lower, deeper' level, but dissuaded his readers from drawing parallels between his wartime experiences and his later tales.

pond with swans on it, a sandpit, a wonderful dell with flowers, a few old-fashioned village houses and, further away, a stream with another mill ....' Further on, he re-emphasized the importance of his childhood memories of the area: 'I was brought up in considerable poverty, but I was happy running about in that country. I took the idea of the Hobbits from the village people and children ....'

Tolkien's literary influences also included northern European myths and sagas such as *Beowulf* and the *Volsunga Saga*. It terms of more modern creativity, Tolkien was inspired by the 19th-century writer and artist William Morris, and liked authors such as Edward Wyke-Smith and H. Rider Haggard. All these various influences, and many others, fed into the works of his rich literary imagination.

THE HOBBIT AND THE LORD OF THE RINGS

I t was in Oxford during the 1920s–40s that Tolkien began the literary masterpieces for which he would achieve enduring fame. One day Tolkien was marking exam papers, and found a blank page. He wrote on the page: 'In a hole in the ground there lived a Hobbit.' He actually did not know what a Hobbit was, but would set about discovering his own creation. He started writing *The Hobbit* in either 1930 or 1931 and was able to show his friend, the writer and philosopher C.S. Lewis, an almost complete manuscript in late 1932.

The Hobbit was written as a story for his children, which Tolkien would read to them on dark winter evenings. It therefore lay dormant for a few years, during which time he published 'The Adventures of Tom Bombadil' (1934), a work of poetry, in *The Oxford Magazine*. The Tom Bombadil character was the lost spirit of the Oxfordshire and Berkshire countryside, a sort of 'Green Man' figure. *The Adventures of Tom Bombadil and Other Verses from the Red Book* was finally published in book form in 1962.

In 1936, everything changed. A family friend of the Tolkiens, Elaine Griffiths, was shown the typed copy of *The Hobbit* and was so impressed with it that she asked Susan Dagnall, who worked at the publisher George Allen & Unwin, to read it. After a favourable review by Stanley Unwin's 10-year-old son, Rayner, they were convinced of the book's power and saleability, and published it in 1937. It has sold more than 100 million copies to date.

The Hobbit was an instant success – the first print run of 1,500 books sold out within two months. Tolkien went to see Stanley Unwin to discuss a follow-up. The manuscripts for his body of works were sent to Unwin. These included *Farmer Giles of Ham, Mr Bliss*, the incomplete story *The Lost Road* and the huge work *The Silmarillion*, but none of these were considered suitable as a sequel. So, in December 1937, Tolkien started what was to become *The Lord of the Rings*, though he did not refer to it by this title for some time.

The book was a vast undertaking. Its hero was to be the son of Bilbo from *The Hobbit*, and he was to be called Bingo – this name came from his children's family of toy koala bears, called the 'Bingos'. Bingo was later renamed Frodo, and became Bilbo's nephew.

The writing of *The Lord of the Rings* during the war years was rather a stop-start affair, but C.S. Lewis encouraged

BELOW: Rayner Unwin. As a boy he was privileged to preview the manuscript of *The Hobbit*, which led to its publication.

ABOVE: Front cover of the first edition of *The Hobbit* by J.R.R. Tolkien, published in 1937. The first printing of 1,500 sold out within weeks.

RIGHT: Title page of *The Fellowship of the Ring*, the first volume of *The Lord of the Rings*, published in 1954.

Tolkien to continue. Writing letters on the progress of the book to his son Christopher, who was in South Africa training pilots, may also have helped spur Tolkien on. In 1944, however, Tolkien was suffering from writer's block. A visit to Birmingham for an old boys' school reunion was to cure this. He revisited the site of his old school in New Street (the school had moved out of the city centre in the 1930s), and here he had a vision of ghosts rising from the pavement. This image freed his mind once again, and he rapidly wrote the chapters 'The Passage of the Marshes' and 'The Black Gate is Closed in the Two Towers'.

By the summer of 1947, *The Lord of the Rings* was almost completed. The son of the publisher Stanley Unwin, Rayner – by this time a student at Oxford – had become friendly with Tolkien and was given an almost complete typed copy of *The Lord of the Rings* to read. Rayner enjoyed it, but was a little uncertain whether it was a book for children or adults. He felt that his father's firm should publish it, but that it should be divided into three books. Tolkien carried on honing and refining *The Lord of the Rings* for the next two years, and then typed up the whole manuscript, completing the process in the autumn of 1949.

THE LORD of the RINGS

The Lord of the Rings was written by J.R.R. Tolkien between 1937 and 1949 and was published in three volumes in 1954 and 1955. The story is set in Tolkien's mythological world of Middle-earth and tells the tale of the destruction of the 'Ring of Power', undertaken by the Fellowship of the Ring. The Fellowship is made up of the Hobbits (Frodo, Sam, Merry and Pippin), Gandalf the Wizard, Gimli the Dwarf, Legolas the Elf, Boromir the man from Gondor and Strider the Ranger. It is considered to be one of the best works of fantasy fiction of the 20th century and was released as three blockbuster films in 2001–03.

FAVOURITE HAUNTS

Many places in the countryside around Oxford were to play their part in Tolkien's fictional world of Middle-earth. In 1932 he purchased a Morris Cowley motor car, which was named Old Jo after the first two letters of the registration plate. After a short time, this car was replaced by a more modern model, which was appropriately called Jo2. The vehicle enabled Tolkien to visit his brother Hilary at his fruit farm in Blackminster, in the Vale of Evesham. On his journey to see his brother, Tolkien would have passed – on the Oxford road just outside Moreton-in-Marsh – the Four Shire Stone, which is likely to be the model for the Three-Farthing Stone marking the centre of his fictional Shire. Also, a short distance off the Oxford road, on the border of Oxfordshire and Warwickshire, stand the Rollright Stones. These are made up of a stone circle called The King's Men, a collapsed portal dolmen tomb known as The Whispering Knights, and a single standing stone called The King Stone. In *The Lord of the Rings*, in the chapter 'Fog on Barrow-Downs', the description of the standing stone and stone circle seems to fit the Rollright Stones quite well, especially on a foggy day in autumn: 'But even as he spoke he turned his glance eastwards, and he saw that on that side the hills were higher and looked down upon them; and all those hills were crowned with green mounds, and on some were standing stones, pointing upwards like jagged teeth out of green gums.'

A few lines further on, the description is expanded: 'In the midst of it there stood a single stone, standing tall under the sun above, and at this hour casting no shadow. It was

ABOVE: The Vale of the White Horse, seen from the Berkshire Downs, could be the inspiration for the Vale of Rohan in *The Lord of the Rings*.

RIGHT: The White Horse chalk figure at Uffington, Oxfordshire, seen from the air. The figure dates from around 1000 BC.

shapeless and yet significant: like a land mark, or a guarding finger, or more like a warning.'

Earlier, in 1912, Tolkien visited Berkshire during his summer break from Exeter College. He went on a walking holiday touring the downs and local villages, while making drawings of the places he passed through. Later, in the 1930s, the Tolkien family would go on trips to the Berkshire Downs above the village of Uffington. This area would have appealed to Tolkien's sense of myth and history. It is rich in Neolithic, Bronze Age and Iron Age monuments, and many of them have legends or tales that come from the Anglo-Saxon period. The most prominent feature is the Uffington White Horse on White Horse Hill. Dating back to the late Bronze Age, the horse is 114m (374ft) long and 33.5m (110ft) deep, and was constructed by filling trenches with chalk rubble. Viewed from the plain below – The Vale of the White Horse – the horse appears to be running on a green background. Significantly, in *The Lord of the Rings* the banner and shield of the House of Eorl (which included all of the kings of Rohan) follows the same pattern – 'a white horse upon green'.

Wayland's Smithy – a Neolithic chambered long barrow – is a short walk along the Ridgeway from White Horse Hill. In *The Lord of the Rings*, when the Hobbits are travelling across the Barrow-downs, they become trapped in a barrow that sounds and feels like Wayland's Smithy: 'To his right there loomed against the westward stars a dark black shape. A great barrow stood there ... Then suddenly he knew that he was imprisoned, caught hopelessly; he was in a barrow.' Such locations illustrate how Britain's rich countryside and heritage fed into Tolkien's imagination, and helped to create some of history's greatest literary landscapes.

ABOVE LEFT: Wayland's Smithy on the Berkshire Downs, showing the entrance to the ancient burial chamber (centre).

ABOVE: The King Stone, one of the Rollright Stones, is on the other side of the road from the ancient stone circle known as The King's Men. The stones are made of oolitic limestone.

MR BLISS

Mr Bliss was written and illustrated by Tolkien for his children. It tells the tale of the eponymous Mr Bliss, an eccentric figure who buys a car and embarks on both adventures and disasters in it. The narrative often reflects some of Tolkien's own driving mishaps, such as one notable trip to see his brother Hilary, when he had a puncture and also drove into a wall. The work was sold to a publisher in 1957, but prohibitive production costs for the colour artwork, and other factors, meant that it remained unpublished until 1982, several years after Tolkien's death.

ABOVE: Cover illustration by Tolkien for the first edition of *Mr Bliss*.

A CIRCLE OF FRIENDS

Tolkien's greatest friendship throughout his life was with his brother. Hilary was Tolkien's steadfast companion from their days shared as young orphans through to their both becoming widowers in later life.

Yet Tolkien developed other friendships of great importance throughout his life, often via his imaginatively conceived clubs. On Tolkien's return to Oxford in 1925, he founded a reading group called the Coalbiters (*Kolbitar* in Icelandic meaning men who lounge so close to the fire in winter that they 'bite the coal'). A group of Oxford dons, they met in the evening several times each term in colleague John Bryson's rooms at Balliol College, to read aloud from Icelandic sagas. The club was similar to the Viking Club formed earlier, in Leeds.

The Coalbiters stopped meeting as a group in the early 1930s, but a new group formed, called The Inklings. This club was originally started by an undergraduate from University College called Edward Tangye Lean, but the name 'Inklings' continued to be used by C.S. Lewis after Lean left Oxford in 1933. The group of men – mostly of the Christian faith – first met in C.S. Lewis's rooms at Magdalen College, and later at the Eagle and Child pub, known to the group as the Bird and Baby, and sometimes at the Lamb and Flag (both pubs stand on St Giles). The main focus of the group was to hear readings of members' unpublished work and give criticism. Tolkien read parts from *The Lord of the Rings* and Lewis from his work *Out of the Silent Planet* (1938). Warren Lewis, a member of the group

RIGHT: The Eagle and Child pub in St Giles, Oxford, was a meeting place for The Inklings, and was known to the group as the Bird and Baby.

FAR RIGHT: The Eagle and Child pub sign.

New Buildings, Magdalen College, built in 1733, where C.S. Lewis had his college rooms. Lewis was a Fellow and Tutor in English Language and Literature.

and C.S. Lewis's elder brother, wrote: 'Properly speaking the Inklings was neither a club nor a literary society, though it partook of the nature of both. There were no rules, officers, agendas, or formal elections.'

The friendship between Tolkien and C.S. Lewis started to drift apart in the late 1930s, partly due to Lewis coming under the strong influence of Charles Williams, who was the editor at the Oxford University Press and a supernatural thriller writer. Williams and Tolkien had an awkward relationship, possibly because of their very different approaches to writing.

Tolkien and Lewis were no longer close by the time Lewis married American writer and divorcee Joy Gresham in 1956. When Lewis died in November 1963, Tolkien wrote to his own son, Michael, about 'Jack' a few days later: 'We were separated first by the sudden apparition of Charles Williams, and then by his marriage. Of which he never told me; I learned of it long after the event. But we owed each a great debt to the other, and that tie with the deep affection that it begot, remains. He was a great man of whom the cold-blooded official obituaries only scraped the surface, in places with injustice.'

J.R.R. TOLKIEN and C.S. LEWIS

Tolkien first met C.S. Lewis in 1926 at an English Faculty meeting at Merton College. They rapidly became great friends. Tolkien and 'Jack' – Lewis had chosen the name for himself at the age of three – would meet in Lewis's rooms at Magdalen College and talk late into the night about their shared interest in Norse mythology, and in May 1927 Lewis joined the Coalbiters. In the early 1930s, Tolkien helped Lewis find his way back to his faith, and to believing in God and Christianity.

In C.S. Lewis's autobiographical book *Surprised by Joy: The Shape of My Early Life*, he talks about his first meeting with Tolkien. He was fascinated by this 'smooth, pale fluent little chap'. But at that time Lewis had two major prejudices: 'At my first coming into the world I had been (implicitly) warned never trust a Papist, and at my first coming into the English Faculty (explicitly) never to trust a philologist. Tolkien was both.' It seems that Lewis overcame both prejudices to become Tolkien's firm friend.

ABOVE: C.S. Lewis, friend to Tolkien and a founder member of The Inklings. The literary group initially met in Lewis's rooms at Magdalen College to read and discuss their latest work.

CDERTON COLLEGE

In 1945, Tolkien was appointed Merton Professor of English Language and Literature, and he taught Old and Middle English. He had rooms in the Fellows' Quadrangle overlooking Merton Field and Christ Church Meadow. It was a lively place socially. Many of the dons were young married men, and it was not uncommon to see their wives and children in and around the college. At the college there were also friends from Tolkien's early days in Oxford, such as Hugo Dyson and Neville Coghill. Tolkien liked the environment of Merton College – it was more relaxed and less formal than it had been at Pembroke College.

The Hobbit was reprinted in 1946; it had literally gone out of print in 1942, when the warehouse in which it was stored was destroyed during an air raid.

In March 1947, the Tolkien family moved out of 20 Northmoor Road to 3 Manor Road, owned by Merton College. It was a three-storey terraced house and much smaller than their previous home. Christopher and Priscilla were still living at home, and Tolkien had a small study in the attic, but the house was far too small for them. The college agreed to move them into a larger house when one became available.

In 1950, a year after the story of *Farmer Giles of Ham* was published, the family finally received a new college house and moved into 99 Holywell Street, a short distance from Manor Road. At the bottom of the garden stood a section of the old town wall and on the other side of the wall was New College Garden. But this house, with its front door opening onto the street, was becoming noisy with the increasing traffic on Holywell Street. Christopher and Priscilla had left home by 1953, so Tolkien and Edith purchased and moved to 76 Sandfield Road, in the Oxford suburb of Headington.

In 1954, the first two books of *The Lord of the Rings* trilogy were published, *The Fellowship of the Ring* and *The Two Towers*. The third book, *The Return of the King*, came out the following year. The books emerged to mixed reviews.

FARMER GILES of HAM

Farmer Giles of Ham was a novel written by Tolkien in 1946–47, although it remained unpublished until 1949. Set in the Dark Ages, it was a far more light-hearted tale than The Lord of the Rings, which Tolkien was writing at the time, and centred around the unlikely hero Farmer Giles, who by an unexpected turn of events becomes a dragon-slayer, more worthy of the title than many of the knights who claim such roles. The book serves as a lighter counterpoint to the darker, more epic mythologies, and shows Tolkien's versatility in the fantasy medium.

BELOW: Merton College Fellows' Quadrangle. Tolkien had rooms at the college and would have known the scene well.

ABOVE: Merton College library, dating from 1373, is the oldest existing academic library in the world.

J.W. Lambert of *The Sunday Times* praised Tolkien's extraordinary imagination, and C.S. Lewis's review was ecstatic about the work, but was attacked by fellow critics because of his friendship with Tolkien. The American critic Edmund Wilson, by contrast, in 1956 considered the whole trilogy to be 'juvenile trash'.

Yet in the same year that Wilson disparaged *The Lord of the Rings*, the work made its first move from the written to the spoken word in the form of a 12-episode radio adaptation on the BBC Third Programme. Radio at the time was still the main home entertainment medium and the Third Programme was the highbrow channel of broadcasting. The book, still only available in hardback, was selling very well and was to be reprinted many times in the coming years, and translated into numerous languages.

Tolkien finally retired from Merton College in 1959, aged 67.

ABOVE: Tolkien photographed in the 1940s by *Time Life* magazine, following the successful publication of *The Hobbit*.

A WORLD-FAMOUS WRITER

After retiring from Merton College, Tolkien had to move all his books out of the college. His study-bedroom at the family home in Sandfield Road was already overflowing with books and papers, but the garage was vacant (he had not owned a car since the 1940s), so this was converted into a library/office. This whole process took several months, and all the carrying and stacking of the books exacerbated his lumbago. Once this was completed, however, he could settle down to working on *The Silmarillion*.

Sandfield Road was a bit off the beaten track, and a long way from any bus services, so Tolkien needed to use taxis to get about. The cost was no longer a concern – the income from his book sales was very good. Tolkien had always been a plain dresser but, as if in testimony to his new-found wealth, he now treated himself to colourful waistcoats.

By the mid 1960s, *The Lord of the Rings* was enjoying worldwide success but not always under the author's or the publisher's control. In 1965 news reached Tolkien that a pirate copy of *The Lord of the Rings* was to be published in America by Ace Books. Eventually the Science Fiction Writers of America persuaded Ace Books to pay Tolkien royalties and not to print any further copies. The authorized version of *The Lord of the Rings* came out in the USA in October 1965, and on the back of all the publicity over the pirate version the book became a huge bestseller.

In 1966, Ronald and Edith celebrated their 50th wedding anniversary with a party at Merton College. One of the highlights of the event was a performance of Tolkien's song cycle *The Road Goes Ever On*. Donald Swann wrote and played the music, and William Elvin sang the words.

As the 1960s progressed, Tolkien's fame grew, as did his fan mail, to which he diligently responded. To help cope with ever-increasing demands on his time he employed a number of part-time secretaries. The decade also brought some unlikely

ABOVE: The cover of *The Lord of the Rings*. Published as a mass-market paperback in 1965, it became a bestseller.

RIGHT: J.R.R. Tolkien photographed in his study in 1961 at the height of his literary career.

associations with Tolkien's work. The hippie 'Flower-Power Movement' proclaimed *The Lord of the Rings* as an important book to read. Most likely this was because the term 'pipe-weed' was used for tobacco in Middle-earth, yet in hippie terminology 'pipe-weed' was taken to mean marijuana, which was often smoked in pipes. There was even a club in London called 'Middle-earth', and a market in Kensington, in London, called 'Gandalf's Garden'.

The Beatles also became inspired by *The Lord of the Rings*, planning to make a film of the book. Paul McCartney was to play Frodo, John Lennon – Gollum, George Harrison – Gandalf, and Ringo Star – Sam. There is a tale that they even approached Stanley Kubrick about directing the film, but the plan eventually fizzled out. Nevertheless, Tolkien had unwittingly become a leading figure in the counter-culture of the time, a phenomenon he probably disliked.

Tolkien's Sandfield Road address and telephone number, which were largely common knowledge, had become a major problem in his life. Fans would knock on the door to get books signed, and they would send him gifts or try to take pictures of him through the windows. Even fans from the United States would phone with questions about his writing, but were often unaware of the time difference between the UK and USA, so these calls would come in the middle of the night. To overcome this problem, Tolkien became ex-directory. In 1968, when Tolkien and Edith were both in their late 70s, they moved to Poole, near Bournemouth in Dorset, to enjoy a more peaceful life.

ABOVE: Tolkien and his wife Edith, a devoted couple, in the garden of their home in Sandfield Road, Oxford, in 1966.

ABOVE: Illustration by Pauline Baynes on the cover of *Bilbo's Last Song*, which also appears in *The Road Goes Ever On* collection.

TOLKIEN'S WORDPLAY

Writing informed many aspects of Tolkien's life in curious and entertaining ways. He often wrote purely for the fun and amusement of his children, creating fictional worlds for them with characters like 'Bill Stickers', the name coming from a sign he had seen on a gate – 'BILL STICKERS WILL BE PROSECUTED'. Bill Stickers was usually being chased by 'Major Road Ahead'. Tolkien's method of writing itself was equally idiosyncratic. He would write at night on the backs of students' old examination papers using pen and ink, replenishing the ink from an inkwell. Then he would rewrite the draft neatly, and finally type up the chapter on his Hammond typewriter.

STORY'S END

R onald and Edith had spent their holidays in Bournemouth, at the Hotel Miramar, for a number of years. Edith suffered from arthritis in her old age and had difficulty climbing stairs, and she felt that the Dorset climate helped ease her stiffness and pain.

On one of their trips to Bournemouth, the couple had visited and viewed 19 Lakeside Road, a bungalow in nearby Poole, and they purchased it the next day. For a traditional couple the modern bungalow had all the latest facilities, such as central heating, two bathrooms and a fitted kitchen, much to Edith's liking. The adjacent garage was converted into Tolkien's study, and Joy Hill, who worked for his publisher Allen & Unwin, would come and help him with his ever-increasing load of international fan mail.

Tolkien and his wife spent three very happy years in the new house, but in November 1971 Edith became seriously ill. She died in a Bournemouth nursing home on 29 November. The bungalow has now been demolished, but the two houses that have replaced it are called Lúthien and Beren, from Tolkien's *The Tale of Beren and Lúthien*.

After Edith's death, Merton College asked Tolkien to become a resident Honorary Fellow of the college, and offered him a flat in one of the college

BELOW: The grave of J.R.R. Tolkien and his wife, Edith, in Wolvercote Cemetery in north Oxford.

Two trees were planted in the University Parks, Oxford, beside the River Cherwell in 1992, to commemorate the centenary of Tolkien's birth. The planting was arranged by the Tolkien Society and the Mythopoeic Society, and the two trees were chosen for their colouration – a silver maple (silver) and a false acacia (gold). These trees represent Telperion and Laurelin, the Two Trees of Valinor mentioned in *The Silmarillion*. Near the trees is a bench bearing a plaque with the following inscription:

IN MEMORY OF J.R.R. TOLKIEN
1892–1973
THIS BENCH AND TWO TREES NEARBY
REPRESENTING TELPERION AND LAURELIN
WERE DONATED BY THE
TOLKIEN CENTENARY CONFERENCE 1992

LEFT: This silver maple tree (left) and a gold tree, a false acacia, planted in the University Parks in 1992, the centenary of Tolkien's birth.

houses, 21 Merton Street. Tolkien accepted, and spent the remaining months of his life in Oxford. In 1972 he was awarded the CBE (Commander of the Order of the British Empire), which was presented to him by the Queen at Buckingham Palace on 28 March.

In August 1973, Tolkien was staying with friends in Bournemouth when he became unwell at a family party. The next day he was taken to hospital, where he developed a severe chest infection and died on 2 September 1973, aged 81.

Tolkien's funeral was held at St Anthony's Church in Headington, Oxford, and a memorial service followed in Merton College Chapel on 17 November. Tolkien and his beloved wife Edith are buried in Wolvercote Cemetery in north Oxford. The grave, visited by many Tolkien fans, bears the inscription 'Edith Mary Tolkien, Lúthien, 1889–1971 and John Ronald Reuel Tolkien, Beren, 1892–1973'. The use of the names Lúthien and Beren once again demonstrates the love the couple had for one another, and poignantly evokes the memory of when Edith danced and sang for Ronald in a woodland glade full of flowering hemlocks, many years previously.

The popularity and power of Tolkien's work has endured well beyond the author's death. Partly through the cinematic treatment of his writings, but also because of the continuing popularity of his books, Tolkien will continue to inspire and entertain new generations of thinkers, dreamers, poets and general readers for decades, if not centuries, to come.

ABOVE: Tolkien standing beside one of his favourite trees, the European Black Pine (*Pinus nigra*), in Oxford's Botanic Garden, on 9 August 1973.

TOLKIEN'S LEGACY

Tolkien's literary legacy is both extensive and influential. Just a cursory glance at a comprehensive Tolkien bibliography, including those works published posthumously, shows a prodigious output of more than 80 works of fiction, poetry, non-fiction (as either writer, translator or editor) and other writings, such as collections of letters. Since his death in 1973, his son Christopher, acting as literary executor, has brought many of his father's unpublished works to his loyal public, including *The Silmarillion*, *The History of Middle-earth*, *The Children of Húrin* and *The Legend of Sigurd and Gudrún*. Such publications have continued to widen our understanding of this great writer.

Tolkien's work has also been significant in a broader cultural and artistic context. Tolkien himself would have probably been largely happy with this situation. Around 1951, he wrote a very long letter about *The Lord of the Rings/The Silmarillion* to Milton Waldman of Collins publishers, in which he stated: 'The cycle should be linked to a majestic whole, and yet leave scope for other minds and hands, wielding paint and music and drama.' 'Other minds and hands' have certainly been inspired by Tolkien's works. In the field of music, songs including Jack Bruce's 'To Isengard' from *Songs for a Tailor* (1969), Led Zeppelin's 'The Battle of Evermore' and 'Misty Mountain Hop' from their fourth, untitled album (1971), and Annie Lennox's 'Into the West' from *Return of the King* (2003) owe a debt to Tolkien. *The Lord of the Rings* also became a stage musical in 2006.

Alongside music, Tolkien's writings have inspired a range of fantasy artworks, some used to illustrate reprints of his books, such as Alan Lee's illustrations

ABOVE: Ian McKellen as the wizard Gandalf in Peter Jackson's 2001 film *The Fellowship of the Ring*, based on Tolkien's book.

RIGHT: The Lady Galadriel played by Cate Blanchett in the film of *The Fellowship of the Ring*.

THE HISTORY of MIDDLE-EARTH

Following Tolkien's death in 1973, his son and literary heir, Christopher Tolkien, over a period of 15 years worked on his father's unpublished tales and background notes, many written before *The Hobbit* and *The Lord of the Rings*. The 12-volume series under the title *The History of Middle-earth* was published between 1983 and 1996. The material dates back to around 1916, some being written while Tolkien was convalescing from trench fever contracted during the Battle of the Somme. It includes *The Book of Lost Tales*. An epic project, *The History of Middle-earth* brings to light the context and thought processes behind Tolkien's greatest works. It also reveals many unseen tales and alternative versions of published passages.

in the 1991 single volume of *The Lord of the Rings* and Ted Nasmith's images in *The Complete Guide to Middle-earth* (2003) by Robert Foster. Of course, many authors themselves have been influenced significantly by Tolkien's writings over the years. Some books are directly related to Tolkien's work, like *There and Back Again* (2000) by Pat Murphy, a science-fiction tale set in outer space but intentionally mirroring *The Hobbit*. Philip Pullman's *His Dark Materials* trilogy takes the reader to a very different set of worlds than Middle-earth, but one of Tolkien's favourite trees in the Oxford Botanic Garden makes an appearance in book three, *The Amber Spyglass* (2000). (Pullman was also a student at Exeter College, Oxford.) More broadly, Tolkien set a benchmark for fantasy writing, and his contextual influence on fantasy works such as the Harry Potter series and *The Hitch Hiker's Guide to the Galaxy*, and even films such as *Star Wars*, is immense. In addition Tolkien's works have inspired and influenced numerous role-playing and computer games and activities.

ABOVE: The cover of a special edition of *The Lord of the Rings*, fully illustrated by Alan Lee, published in 1991 to celebrate the centenary, in 1992, of Tolkien's birth.

BELOW RIGHT: Gollum, as featured in *The Two Towers*, Peter Jackson's 2002 film.

BELOW: Elijah Wood (right) and Sean Astin played the Hobbits Frodo and Sam in the film *The Fellowship of the Ring*.

AROUND OXFORD

Oxford is one of the most beautiful cities in Britain, and for the modern Tolkien enthusiast it has much to offer in terms of sightseeing and education. Oxford city centre is crammed with colleges and fine buildings bearing towers, battlements, domes and stone carvings, evoking a fantasy skyline. This vista was very different from the rural hamlet of Sarehole and the Victorian/Edwardian Birmingham of Tolkien's boyhood. The part this townscape played in the fictional world of Middle-earth is hard to determine, as Hobbits are very rural-living creatures, but Tolkien did say that his mythical Sauron's temple to Morgoth on the island of Númenor looked like the Radcliffe Camera.

Some of Tolkien's favourite meeting places are still open for business. In the 1940s, Tolkien would meet C.S. Lewis and Charles Williams for a drink in the White Horse public house on Broad Street. There he would sometimes read them a chapter from his ongoing work *The Lord of the Rings*, as he noted in one of his letters to his son Christopher on 18 April 1944: 'I hope to see C.S.L. and Charles W. tomorrow morning and read my next chapter – on the passage of the Dead Marshes and the approach to the Gates of Mordor, which I have now practically finished.' Inside, the pub is very small, and other customers would have easily overheard the reading. One of the chapters in *The Lord of the Rings* is called 'At the Sign of the Prancing Pony' – the pub sign does indeed look like a prancing pony.

Another Tolkien landmark is the Eastgate Hotel where, in the 1930s, Tolkien and Lewis would meet on Monday mornings for a chat and a beer.

BELOW: Radcliffe Camera.

It is Lewis's booming voice that is credited as the root of Treebeard's equally sonorous voice in *The Lord of the Rings*. Treebeard is an Ent, a tree-like creature that herds and protects the trees in the Forest of Fangorn. C.S. Lewis had rooms in New Buildings at Magdalen College, where he lived on weekdays during term-time. Tolkien would visit Lewis there in his large sitting-room on occasions. They would talk late into the night, in a fog of tobacco smoke (both men were pipe smokers), about their shared interest in Norse mythology. Years later, in the 1970s while living at 21 Merton Street after the death of Edith, Tolkien would frequently dine at the Eastgate Hotel, which by this time had moved upmarket from the days when he would meet his friend there.

During his time at Pembroke College, Tolkien would have seen Tom Tower, one of Oxford's great landmarks, standing on the other side of St Aldates from Pembroke. The tower is the main entrance to Christ Church; the lower section is of 15th-century origin, while the upper section was designed by Sir Christopher Wren and completed in 1682. The tower houses the great Tom Bell, which rings the curfew in the evening to call the students back into the college.

Oxford's famous Botanic Garden was also frequented by Tolkien, who appreciated its peaceful atmosphere and aesthetic mood. The garden is the oldest botanic garden in Britain. Known to be one of Tolkien's favourite trees, a European Black Pine

(*Pinus nigra*) stands in the garden, a short walk from 21 Merton Street. The last photograph of Tolkien was taken standing by the tree in August 1973 (see page 25).

Number 20 Northmoor Road has a particular resonance in Tolkien's life. It was home for the Tolkien family from 1930 to 1947, and most of *The Hobbit* and *The Lord of the Rings* were written during his time there. The previous owner of that particular house was Sir Basil Blackwell, the son of the founder of Blackwell's bookshop in Broad Street, Oxford. At that time, Sir Basil was

TOLKIEN'S CHURCHES

Tolkien was a very devout Roman Catholic, and attended St Aloysius Church on the Woodstock Road. Cardinal Newman had preached there in the 19th century, and he had founded the Birmingham Oratory, where Tolkien had worshipped when he was living in Edgbaston. The church was built in 1875, and at the time that Tolkien worshipped there it was served by the Jesuit Fathers. Cardinal Newman had always dreamt of it becoming an oratory, and in 1993 it did indeed become the Oxford Oratory. Tolkien also attended St Gregory and St Augustine, another church on the Woodstock Road, in the district of Upper Wolvercote. While living in Sandfield Road, the Tolkiens worshipped at the nearby St Anthony's Church.

the owner of the family publishing and bookshop empire. He had published one of Tolkien's poems, 'Goblin's Feet', in *Oxford Poetry* in 1915.

Tolkien took his final examinations for the Honours School of English Language and Literature at the Sheldonian Theatre on Broad Street in June 1915. The Sheldonian Theatre was built in 1664–69, and it was the first building designed by Sir Christopher Wren, who at the time was a Professor of Astronomy at Oxford. It was commissioned by Gilbert Sheldon, hence its name, who provided the £14,500 towards its building.

Oxford is, as we have seen, rich in landmarks of Tolkien's life. A day spent in the city taking in these sights can help to enhance our understanding of Tolkien's life and influences. It also raises the possibility of making even more connections with the life and work of one of the greatest literary minds the world has ever known.

RIGHT: Martyrs' Memorial.

PLACES TO VISIT IN OXFORD

Listed here are details of a selection of places that Tolkien knew. Many Oxford colleges are open at certain times, generally in the afternoons. Some colleges may only be seen on an organized tour, and some are not open to the public. It is best to contact individual colleges to check before you visit. The university museums and other buildings such as the Sheldonian Theatre are also open to the public, but check opening times before visiting. The Radcliffe Camera is a reading room of the Bodleian Library and very rarely open to visitors.

Balliol College, Broad Street www.balliol.ox.ac.uk
Botanic Garden, High Street www.botanic-garden.ox.ac.uk
Carfax Tower, Queen Street
   www.citysightseeingoxford.com/carfax_tower

ABOVE: Sheldonian Theatre.

ABOVE: Tom Tower, Christ Church.

Christ Church, St Aldates www.chch.ox.ac.uk
Corpus Christi College, Merton Street www.ccc.ox.ac.uk
Eagle and Child, and Lamb and Flag public houses, St Giles
Eastgate Hotel, on the corner of Merton Street and High Street
Examination Schools, High Street www.admin.ox.ac.uk/schools
Exeter College and Chapel, Turl Street www.exeter.ox.ac.uk
Magdalen College, High Street www.magd.ox.ac.uk
Martyrs' Memorial, Magdalen Street
Merton College and Chapel, Merton Street
   www.merton.ox.ac.uk
Old Ashmolean Building (home to the Museum of the History of
   Science), Broad Street www.mhs.ox.ac.uk
Pembroke College, Pembroke Square www.pmb.ox.ac.uk
St Aloysius Roman Catholic Church, on Woodstock Road next to
   Somerville College www.oxfordoratory.org.uk
Sheldonian Theatre, Broad Street www.sheldonian.ox.ac.uk
University Parks and Mesopotamia, off South Parks Road
White Horse public house, Broad Street
Wolvercote Cemetery, on the Banbury Road just past the
   roundabout with the A40

ABOVE: Botanic Garden.   OPPOSITE: Map of Oxford city centre.

Other Places to Visit

Rollright Stones: located north of Oxford off the A44 between
Chipping Norton and Moreton-in-Marsh; follow the signs for Great
Rollright and look out for the signs to the Rollright Stones.
www.rollrightstones.co.uk

White Horse Hill and Wayland's Smithy: these two sites are located
south of Oxford about a 30-minute drive away and are open 365 days
a year. The closest town to them is Wantage and then it is a short drive
along the B4507. www.wiltshirewhitehorses.org.uk

Sarehole Mill: located in the Birmingham suburb of Hall Green.
www.bmag.org.uk/sarehole-mill
The mill is in the centre of The Shire Country Park, and Moseley Bog is
a short walk from the mill. www.birmingham.gov.uk/shirecountrypark

The Tolkien Society

The Tolkien Society was founded by Vera Chapman in
1969 to further interest in the life and works of Tolkien.
Registered as an educational charity in the UK, it has
a worldwide membership. Find out more through the
website, which provides members and non-members
with general information about the society and the
world of Tolkien, and further educational resources.
www.tolkiensociety.org
Hon. Pres.: the late Professor J.R.R. Tolkien, CBE In Perpetuo
Hon. Vice Pres.: Priscilla Tolkien
Registered Charity No. 273809

Websites

www.tolkiensociety.org
www.planet-tolkien.com
www.theonering.com

ACKNOWLEDGEMENTS

Written by Robert S. Blackham. The author has asserted his
moral rights.
Edited by Shelley Grimwood.
Designed by Glad Stockdale.
Cover designed by Sophie Holford.
Map by The Map Studio, Romsey, Hampshire, based on
cartography © George Philip Ltd.
Picture research by Robert S. Blackham and Jan Kean.

Illustrations reproduced by kind permission of Robert S.
Blackham except for: Exeter College: 13tr; Getty Images:
21cr (Time Life Pictures); Martin Latham FC
background; Pitkin Publishing: 18br, 20, 21cl, 28,
29cr, 30 both, 31 both, 32 (Neil Jinkerson); Random
House: 23br; Rex Features: 24, 29tl (Nigel R.
Barklie); TopFoto: FC foreground 15tr (The Granger
Collection), 14 22cb 23t (ArenaPAL/Pamela
Chandler) 15tl 25br(National Pictures), 22cl.

Quotations reprinted by permission of: p13 panel
HarperCollins Publishers Ltd © 2003 *Tolkien and
the Great War*, John Garth; p13 *The Guardian* ©
Guardian News and Media Ltd 1991; pp16–17 *The
Fellowship of the Ring* © The J.R.R. Tolkien 1967
Discretionary Settlement and The Tolkien Trust 1954,
1966 (HarperCollins Publishers Ltd, J.R.R. Tolkien); p19
C.S. Lewis: Life, Works and Legacy, Bruce L. Edwards
© 2007, reproduced with permission of ABC-CLIO, Santa
Barbara, CA; p19 panel HarperCollins Publishers Ltd
© 1990 *C.S. Lewis: A Biography*, A.N. Wilson; pp19,
26, 28 *The Letters of J.R.R. Tolkien* © The J.R.R. Tolkien
Copyright Trust 1981 (HarperCollins Publishers Ltd,
Humphrey Carpenter and Christopher Tolkien, ed.).

Every effort has been made to contact copyright
holders and the publisher will be pleased to rectify any
omissions in future editions.

Publication in this form © Pitkin Publishing 2011. No part of
this publication may be reproduced by any means without
the permission of Pitkin Publishing and the copyright holders.

Printed in Great Britain.
ISBN: 978-1-84165-329-7   1/11